A Children's Book About

CHEATING

Managing Editor: Ellen Klarberg
Copy Editor: Annette Gooch
Editorial Assistant: Lana Eberhard
Art Director: Jennifer Wiezel
Production Artist: Gail Miller
Illustration Designer: Bartholomew
Inking Artist: Berenice Happé Iriks
Coloring Artist: Berenice Happé Iriks
Lettering Artist: Linda Hanney
Typographer: Communication Graphics

A Children's Book About

CHEATING

By Joy Berry

GROLIER ENTERPRISES CORP.

This book is about Sam and his sister Maggie.

Reading about Sam and Maggie can help you understand and deal with **cheating**.

Most people want to win the games they play. But everyone cannot win. If someone is going to win, someone else must lose.

No one likes to lose.

When you lose, you might think you have lost because you are not as smart as those who win.

Losing might make you feel dumb.

When you do not feel good about yourself,
you might think you cannot do anything
well. You might feel that you will never win.

If you lose often, you might begin to think you must cheat in order to win.

You are cheating when you sneak and break the rules of a game.

Do not cheat in order to win.

There are other things you can do to make sure you win at least some of the time:
- Play with people your age or younger.
- Play with people who are equal to you in experience and ability.

Play "equal-chance" games with people who are older than you.

Equal-chance games are won with luck rather than skill or practice.

Do not always play games you know you
will lose.

Play games you know you will have a
chance to win.

Know the rules of a game before you play it.
Make sure the people who play with you
know the rules.

Then make sure that everyone playing the
game agrees to follow the rules.

Follow the rules when you play a game.

Do not do anything that is against the rules.

Do not try to change the rules in the middle of the game.

Remember these things:
- You play for fun when you play a game.
- Having a good time is more important than winning.

Concentrate on having fun and try not to worry about winning or losing.

If people cheat during a game, talk with them about it in a nice way.

Tell them you know they are cheating and ask them to stop.

Stop playing with people who continue to cheat.

Remember, no one can win all the time.
When you lose a game:
- Do not think of yourself as a loser.
- Do not think you will never win.
- Do not give up or stop trying.
- Think about the things you are good at.
- Remember the times you have won.

It is important to treat other people the way you want to be treated.

If you do not want other people to cheat, you must not cheat.